ONE GIANT LEAP

Robert Burleigh   PAINTINGS BY Mike Wimmer

PUFFIN BOOKS
AN IMPRINT OF PENGUIN GROUP (USA)

PUFFIN BOOKS
Published by the Penguin Group
Penguin Group (USA) LLC
375 Hudson Street
New York, New York 10014

USA * Canada * UK * Ireland * Australia
New Zealand * India * South Africa * China

penguin.com
A Penguin Random House Company

First published in the United States of America by Philomel Books,
a division of Penguin Young Readers Group, 2009
Published by Puffin Books, an imprint of Penguin Young Readers Group, 2014

Text copyright © 2009 by Robert Burleigh
Illustrations copyright © 2009 by Mike Wimmer

THE LIBRARY OF CONGRESS HAS CATALOGED THE PHILOMEL BOOKS EDITION AS FOLLOWS:
Burleigh, Robert. One giant leap / Robert Burleigh ; illustrated by Mike Wimmer.
p. cm.
ISBN 978-0-399-23883-3(hc)
1. Project Apollo (U.S.)—History—Juvenile literature. 2. Space flight to the moon—History—Juvenile literature.
I. Wimmer, Mike, ill. II. Title. TL789.8.U6A52423   2008   629.45′4—dc22   2008015695

Puffin Books ISBN 978-0-14-751165-2

Printed in the United States of America

15 17 19 20 18 16 14

For Aiden and Austin Scott

(along with Robin, Ryan, Sue and Ralph)

R. B.

This book is dedicated to the men and women who look to the heavens, not just for inspiration but for a destination. I would like to recognize the following people for their invaluable help with research and getting the facts straight, which helped bring this historic event to life: Max Ary; J. Milt Heflin, Associate Director (Technical), Office of the Director, NASA–Johnson Space Center; Mike Gentry, Media Resource Center, NASA–Johnson Space Center; Suzette Ellison, Oklahoma Science Museum.

M. W.

They orbit in sight of each other one last time.

Then the *Eagle* begins to descend—

To where no human has ever been.

To the moon.

The *Eagle* is like a gold-speckled bug falling out of the sky—

Its odd-shaped body plastered with many boxes,

Its outer walls thinner than human skin.

The spacecraft's spindly legs poke out as it rides on its back.

At 8,000 feet, it tilts and straightens.

Brakes its descent. Slows.

Drifts down through space.

The astronauts look out at last.

Neil Armstrong. Buzz Aldrin.

They stand upright before two small windows.

Their eyes widen.

Look—rushing up toward them—

The moon!

It is gray, it is brown, it is blue-edged.

Its billion-year-old landscape is cracked and scarred,

Its surface gouged and cratered and pitted with tiny holes,

Like a battlefield from some ancient war.

The radio voice crackles from Earth, 240,000 miles away:

"*EAGLE*, HOUSTON: YOU ARE *GO* FOR LANDING."

Armstrong tenses forward, feeling the seconds tick,

Aware that the fuel is sinking toward zero.

Timing is everything.

His gaze darts between nearby rows of switches

And the strange world below.

Dark ridges rise like forbidding walls,

Spidery shadows creep in the rising sunlight,

Boulders loom up as big as cars.

He glances again at the flashing dial: *fuel running short*.

Where can he land?

"EAGLE: 90 SECONDS OF DESCENT FUEL LEFT."

Armstrong hears the warning.

Now. All he has ever learned is focused on this.

Nothing matters but this exact moment.

Aldrin's nonstop voice calls out altitude numbers:

"Forty feet, thirty-five, thirty . . ."

Down they move, down and down.

Fast enough to conserve precious fuel.

Slow enough to land somewhere safely.

He hopes.

The *Eagle* dips. Hovers. Zigs. Zags.

Dances over its own dark shadow.

The seconds tick toward eternity. Time stops.

Clouds of moondust swirl like blackening fog.

An almost terrifying blindness.

And then—with only the very slightest bump—

The small craft touches down.

Whew!

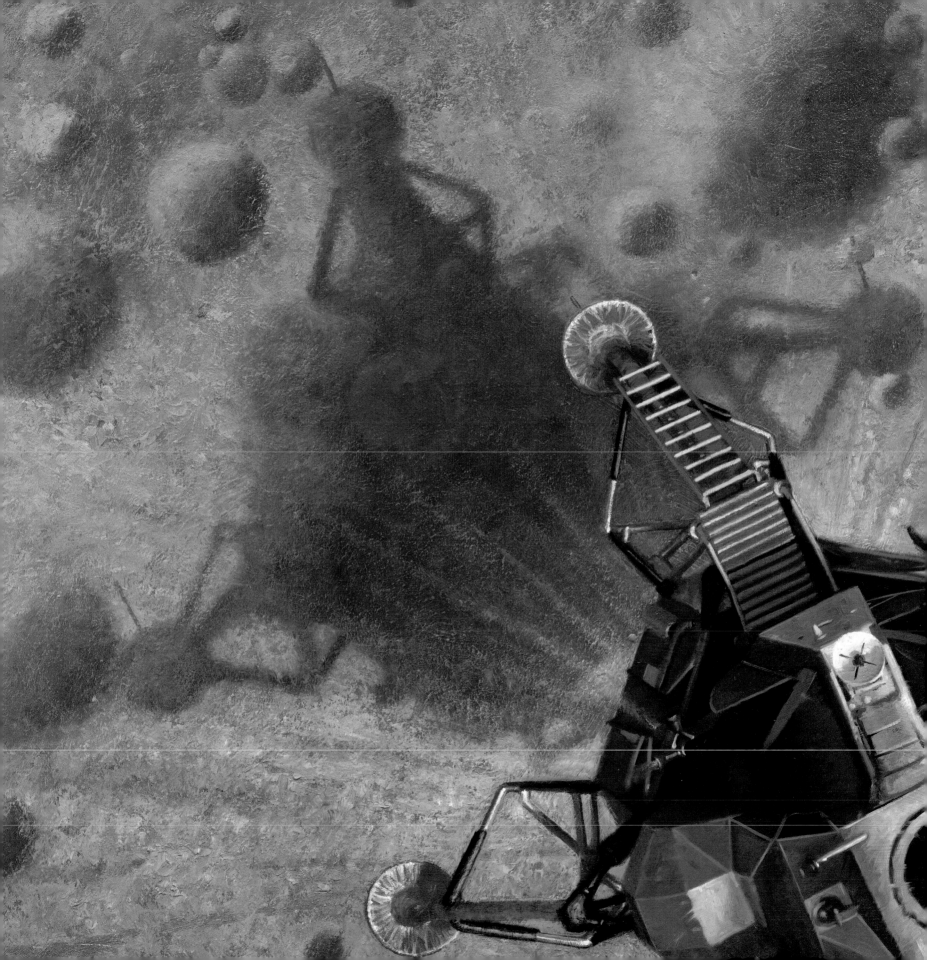

"The *Eagle* has landed."

High overhead, Michael Collins listens, but cannot see.

They made it. They made it!

The *Columbia* orbits—and waits.

Collins has waited a lifetime for this.

Yet for him, the waiting is not over.

In Houston, on Earth, hundreds in the control room break into wild cheers.

The first humans on the moon!

But in this other place it is very quiet.

It is lunar morning on the Sea of Tranquility.

Armstrong lets out another deep breath and turns.

He raises his gloved hand and meets Aldrin's gloved hand halfway.

We did it. We're here.

Exploration time!

Armstrong and Aldrin add still more to their spacesuits.

There are new overshoes and heavier gloves,

A visored helmet to protect against sunlight,

And an oxygen-filled backpack thick as a sofa pillow.

They pause to gaze out:

An endless, mysterious wasteland,

Whose distant hills are as sharply outlined as nearby stones.

No water. No wind. No sound.

No life at all.

Unbelievable.

A hatch opens.

Armstrong, on all fours, crawls through its small space.

He moves awkwardly in his "moon cocoon."

Outside, on the narrow porch,

Where a ladder is attached to one landing leg,

He climbs to the bottom rung and stops.

A TV camera, placed in the *Eagle*'s hatchway, is pointed down.

Armstrong knows that back on Earth,

Hundreds of millions of people are watching.

He jumps to the landing leg's round footpad.

He holds on. He pauses. He points his foot and steps off.

The surface is as fine as powdered charcoal.

The treads of his boot leave a perfectly crisp print in the dust.

On the weatherless moon, it will last for millions of years.

His voice sounds staticky and far away:

"That's one small step for man—one giant leap for mankind."

In orbit, Michael Collins listens. And waits.

Now it is Buzz Aldrin's turn.

He climbs down, feeling full of goose pimples.

Together the astronauts go moon-walking.

Flexing their toes and ankles, they walk stiffly,

As if navigating inside a rigid balloon.

But moving about is easier than they expect.

They twirl like slow-motion tiptoe dancers.

They jog. They kangaroo-hop,

Like two boys bouncing on a trampoline.

Because of the moon's lesser gravity, they feel light as air.

Armstrong checks the time. They must hurry.

They have just two hours on this strange and beautiful world.

They use long metal tongs to collect rocks.

Some are slippery with dust.

Some sparkle. Some look tan or even purple.

The rocks go into two large boxes that scientists will open back on Earth.

They try to plant the American flag.

But underneath its surface dust, the moon is like steel.

They jab the pole into the hard crust.

They twist and turn, leaning with all their might.

At last they are able to balance the staff—just barely.

A rod across the top keeps the flag unfurled.

Then *click*. Armstrong takes a picture of Aldrin saluting the flag.

A surprise call comes from the President:

"For a priceless moment, all the people on this earth are truly one."

A tightness rises in the throats of the astronauts.

They feel part of something so much larger than themselves.

Yet soon it is over. They are inside again.

This world is not theirs. Not their own.

Streaks of dirt cover their spacesuits.

The smell of the moondust hits them as they remove their helmets.

"Like spent cap pistols," they tell each other.

They have been awake for eighteen hours straight, but it feels like much more.

Can they sleep now? Maybe.

It is shivery cold in the cramped *Eagle*.

Aldrin curls up on the floor.

Armstrong lies in a hammock stretched across the room.

Exhausted.

He looks up. Above him, there is an unshuttered porthole.

The earth stares down. "A big blue eyeball," he thinks.

He blinks back at the bright blue eye.

Then turns. And tries to sleep.

July 21. Unease. Uncertainty.

This is the part they are most afraid of.

This is the place where things can go terribly wrong.

Armstrong and Aldrin stand quietly in the tiny cockpit.

Liftoff in one minute. Away from here—*maybe*.

The *Eagle* will split into two parts.

The upper half must fly up.

The lower will stay on the moon—a permanent monument.

Will the engine light? Will it keep on burning?

They try to ease their worries—but there is no escape from this.

No backing up. No doing it again. No second try.

They know one thing only: failure means death.

The second hand winds down. Now or never.

Aldrin's voice cuts into the awful stillness.

"Three, two, one . . . ascent . . ."

At first—a frightening pause. What is happening?

Then bang! Whoosh! Zoom!

It feels as if the floor is coming up at them.

The *Eagle*'s top half rises like a fast-moving elevator.

Its engine leaves a trail of wide, white light.

The *Eagle* soars skyward, silently, faster and faster:

Fifty miles up. Almost a mile a second!

Aldrin glances sideways. Nods and grins.

Into moon orbit. On our way.

He scans the sky and sees—only blackness.

The *Columbia* has been circling now for over twenty hours.

From the far side of the moon,

Collins cannot even radio back to people on Earth.

He squints through the sextant's eyepiece again.

There! A tiny blinking light in the darkness!

He locks his computer on the distant speck, tracking its approach.

The *Eagle* keeps climbing and climbing. Up and up.

It is like an intricate dance: *Columbia* leads; *Eagle* follows.

All at speeds of over 3,000 miles an hour!

Now they fly in perfect formation. Closer. Closer.

Collins punches hundreds of keystrokes to make the docking work.

They touch. They connect. The capture latches snap shut.

A small door opens into a tunnel.

Look who's here! Welcome!

Armstrong and Aldrin come floating through . . .

It is the final orbit around the moon . . .

Can a photo capture the wonder of what they've seen? Not likely.

Still, the astronauts hover beside the *Columbia*'s windows taking pictures.

The spacecraft accelerates.

It curls around the moon's far edge.

It is flung free like the tail-end skater in a game of crack-the-whip.

It soars into the emptiness of space.

The astronauts look back with a sad–happy feeling.

Hours go by. They can rest at last.

They sleep. Read. Talk. Play music.

Sometimes they glimpse the slowly receding moon.

Was it all a dream? No, we were there. We were there!

But mostly their eyes are fixed on another place:

Blue, white, light brown and shining below them.

They want that now. More than anything.

A planet of oceans and rivers. Of grass and green hills.

A world of trees and family and friends.

A place called Earth: fragile, beautiful, home.

A man on the moon! On the moon! The moon!

It was July 20, 1969. For one miraculous moment, the playfulness of nursery rhymes, the fantasy of science fiction, and the reality of true science were joined. We—a billion, more or less, of Earth's inhabitants—watched on snow-flecked, black-and-white television screens as a stiff figure climbed down a ladder and planted a boot in the soft dust of another world.

How did it come about? When President John F. Kennedy proclaimed in the early 1960s that America would land an astronaut on the moon within the decade, it sounded to many like an unreachable dream or, at most, simple politics. And in one sense, it was. Kennedy's promise came during the Cold War between the United States and the Soviet Union. The Russians had earlier sent a cosmonaut around the earth. America responded with its own space program. The big prize was the moon. And the race was on!

The amount of money, the people-hours, the planning, the trials and errors, and the dogged belief of thousands of men and women—all that went into that first step in the soft dust—is beyond the scope of this book. But the result of that dedicated effort—America's moon landing—may well be the single most concentrated and successful effort to achieve one great goal in human history.

Where the United States space program is going today is unclear. Our technological power has increased to an amazing degree in the past half-century. Today one tiny chip can hold far more information and facilitate far more activities than even the hugest, bulkiest computer a half-century ago.

What we do with this new power, in regard to space travel, is still to be decided. What is our next destination? There are millions of galaxies in the universe besides ours (the Milky Way). Traveling to one of them—perhaps at the speed of light!—may seem impossible now. But remember: Space exploration of any kind once seemed impossible. So don't be too sure.

One thing, though, is certain. Regardless of what occurs in the future, nothing can diminish the heroic achievement and sublime beauty of the moment when humans first landed on Earth's one and only moon.

Robert Burleigh

was born in Chicago, Illinois, and received his bachelor's degree from DePauw University and an MA in humanities from the University of Chicago. Since the early 1990s, Robert has written more than thirty children's books. In addition to his writing work, he paints under the pseudonym Burleigh Kronquist. His work has been shown all over the country, including Chicago and New York.

Visit Robert Burleigh online at **www.robertburleigh.com.**

Mike Wimmer

grew up in Muskogee, Oklahoma. An active imagination and an interest in comic books and adventure stories fueled Mike's creative side at a young age. Mike later studied art at the University of Oklahoma, which provided an opportunity to learn from Don Ivan Punchatz at his famous Sketch Pad Studio in Arlington, Texas.

Visit Mike Wimmer online at **www.mikewimmer.com.**